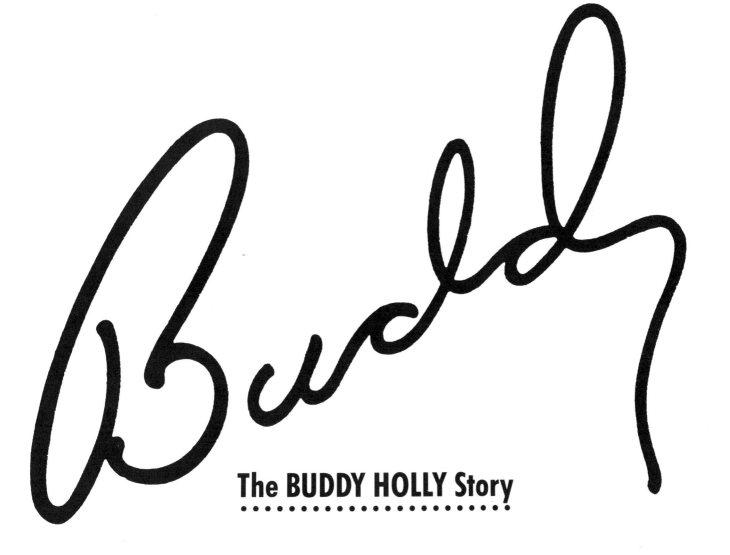

The BUDDY HOLLY Story

Wise Publications
London/New York/Sydney

Exclusive distributors:
Music Sales Limited
8/9 Frith Street,
London W1V 5TZ, England.
Music Sales Pty Limited
120 Rothschild Avenue,
Rosebery, NSW 2018,
Australia.

This book © Copyright 1991 by
Wise Publications
Order No. AM83486
ISBN 0.7119.2531.3

The original London cast recording of
'Buddy: The Buddy Holly Story' is available
on First Night Records (Queue 1).

Book designed by Pearce Marchbank Studio
Compiled by Peter Evans
Production photographs by Eric Thompson

Printed in the United Kingdom by
J.B. Offset Printers (Marks Tey) Limited, Marks Tey, Essex.

Music Sales' complete catalogue lists thousands of titles and is
free from your local music shop, or direct from Music Sales Limited.
Please send a cheque/postal order for £1.50 for postage to
Music Sales Limited, 8/9 Frith Street, London W1V 5TZ.

Your Guarantee of Quality
As publishers, we strive to produce every book to the highest
commercial standards.
The book has been carefully designed to minimise awkward page
turns, and to make playing from it a real pleasure.
Particular care has been given to specifying acid-free, neutral-
sized paper which has not been chlorine bleached but produced with
special regard for the environment. Throughout, the printing and
binding have been planned to ensure a sturdy, attractive
publication which should give years of enjoyment.
If your copy fails to meet our high standards, please inform us
and we will gladly replace it.

That'll Be The Day

Words & Music by Norman Petty, Buddy Holly & Jerry Allison

4

you say, good-bye, Yes,__ that-'ll be the day, when you make me cry, Ah, you say you're gon-na leave,   you

To Verse 2

know it's a lie, 'cause   that -'ll be the day_____ when I die.__ Well, __ when I die.__

When Cu-pid shot his dart,   He shot it at your heart, So if we ev-er part and   I leave you,

To Chorus

You say you told me 'an you   told me bold-ly,   That some day, well, I'll   be   through. Well,

D.S. al Fine

Everyday

Words & Music by Charles Hardin & Norman Petty

do you ev - er long for   true love from   me? _____

Ev - 'ry   day   it's a - get - tin' clos - er,   Go - ing fast - er

than a roll - er - coast - er;   Love like   yours will   tru - ly come my   way. _____

way. _____

8

Peggy Sue

Words & Music by Jerry Allison, Norman Petty & Buddy Holly

I love you, ___ Peg - gy Sue, ___ With a love so

rare and true, ___ Oh Peg - gy, ___ My Peg - gy Sue; ___

Oh, well, I love you, gal, ___ Yes, I want you, Peg - gy Sue. ___

D.S. al Fine | *Fine*

11

I'm Looking For Someone To Love

Words & Music by Buddy Holly & Norman Petty

Words Of Love

Words & Music by Buddy Holly

Hold me close and tell me how you feel, ___

Tell me love is real; ___

Oh, ___ Oh;

15

Oh Boy

Words & Music by Sunny West, Bill Tilghman & Norman Petty

lit -tle bit o' lov -in' makes ev -'ry-thing right, An' I'm gon -na see my

ba -by to -ni -ght! All o' my love, all o' my kiss -in',

You don't know what you been miss -in', Oh Boy! __ (Oh Boy!) When you're with me, __ Oh Boy! __

__ (Oh Boy!) The world can see __ that you were meant for

Not Fade Away

Words & Music by Charles Hardin & Norman Petty

True Love Ways

Words & Music by Buddy Holly & Norman Petty

22

Listen To Me

Words & Music by Charles Hardin & Norman Petty

Moderato, not too slowly, with a Rockin' beat

be _____ near - er each day, _____ My on - ly

dar - ling, lis - ten close - ly to me. _____

me. _____

Chantilly Lace

Words & Music by J. P. Richardson

28

VERSE 3 (patter) *Woo ha ha ha ha ha honey, you're tearin' me up on this telephone.*
I swear I don't know what I'm gonna do with you, you yap and yap
and yap and yap and yap but when you break it all down you know
what I like.   *(to CHORUS)*

Rave On

Words & Music by Sunny West, Bill Tilghman & Norman Petty

Well - ell - ell, RAVE ON! It's a cra - zy feel - in' and I know it's —

got me reel - in', I'm' so glad that you're re-veal - in' your love for

me! RAVE ON, RAVE ON and tell _ me, Tell me not _

— to be lone - ly, Tell me you love me on - ly,

RAVE ON to me. Well - ell - ell RAVE ON to me.

31

It's So Easy

Words & Music by Buddy Holly & Norman Petty

Moderately bright rock beat

It's so eas-y to fall in love, It's so eas-y to fall in love.

Peo-ple tell me love's for fools, So here I go break-ing all of the rules

It seems so eas-y, (Hum), so dog-gone eas-y;

Well All Right

Words & Music by Jerry Allison, Buddy Holly, Joe Maudlin & Norman Petty

CHORUS

___ when lights ___ are low. ___
___ that comes ___ their way. ___

Well all right, ___   well all right, ___

Oh, we'll live and love with all our might, Well all right, ___   Well all right,

Our ___ life - time love will be all right, well all right be all right. ___

1.
To Verse

2.

35

Peggy Sue Got Married

Words & Music by Buddy Holly

Maybe Baby

Words & Music by Charles Hardin & Norman Petty

Moderate Country beat

May-be, ba-by, I'll have you.____ May-be ba-by, you'll be true.____

May-be, ba-by, I'll have you____ for me.____

It's fun-ny, hon-ey; you don't care.____ You nev-er lis-ten to my prayer.____
Instrumental

Maybe, baby, you will love me some day._____ Well, you are the one____ that makes me sad,____ and you are the one____ that makes me glad.____ When some-day you want me,____ I'll be there. Just wait and see.___ Maybe, baby, I'll have you.____ Maybe, baby, you'll be true.____ Maybe, baby,

I'll have you___ for me.___ me.

May-be, ba-by, I'll have you.___ May-be, ba-by, you'll be true.___

May-be, ba-by, I'll have you___ for___ me.

Repeat and fade

40